Country ABCs

Russia ABCs

A Book About the People and Places of Russia

Written by Ann Berge   •   Illustrated by Jeff Yesh

Special thanks to our advisers for their expertise:
James von Geldern, Ph.D.
Professor of Russian
Macalester College, St. Paul, Minnesota

Susan Kesselring, M.A., Literacy Educator
Rosemount-Apple Valley-Eagan (Minnesota) School District

PICTURE WINDOW BOOKS
Minneapolis, Minnesota

Managing Editor: Bob Temple
Creative Director: Terri Foley
Editor: Nadia Higgins
Editorial Adviser: Andrea Cascardi
Copy Editor: Laurie Kahn
Designer: John Moldstad
Page production: Picture Window Books
Prototype: Ann Berge, Anne Goodner
The illustrations in this book were prepared digitally.

Picture Window Books
5115 Excelsior Boulevard
Suite 232
Minneapolis, MN 55416
1-877-845-8392
www.picturewindowbooks.com

Printed in the United States of America.

Library of Congress Cataloging-in-Publication Data
Berge, Ann.
Russia ABCs : a book about the people and places of Russia /
written by Ann Berge ; illustrated by Jeff Yesh.
p. cm. — (Country ABCs)
Summary: An alphabetical exploration of the people,
geography, animals, plants, history, and culture of Russia.
Includes bibliographical references and index.
ISBN 1-4048-0284-3 (Reinforced Library Binding)
1. Russia (Federation)—Juvenile literature. 2. English language—
Alphabet—Juvenile literature. [1. Russia (Federation) 2. Alphabet.]
I. Yesh, Jeff, 1971- ill. II. Title. III. Series.
DK510.23 .B47 2004
947—dc22
2003016521

Privyet! (pree-VYET)

That means "hi" in Russian. Russia is the biggest country in the world. It crosses two continents, Europe and Asia. Almost 145 million people live in Russia. It ranks 8th in world population.

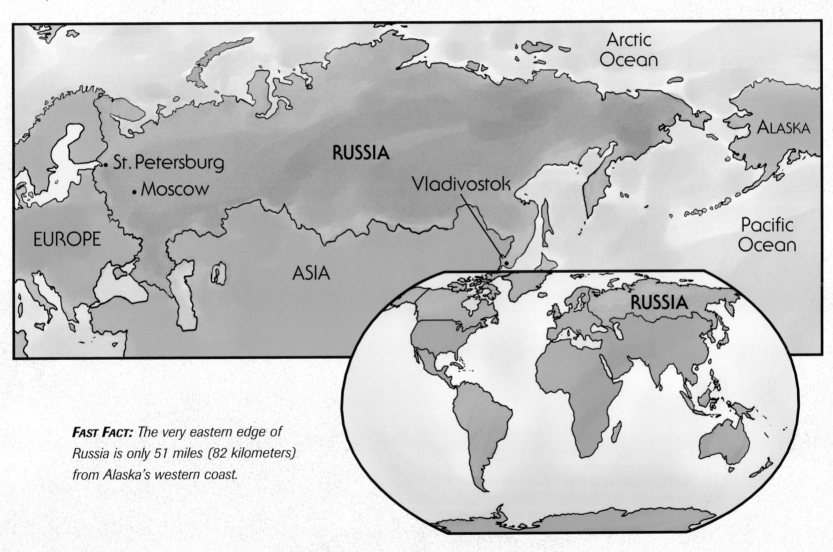

FAST FACT: The very eastern edge of Russia is only 51 miles (82 kilometers) from Alaska's western coast.

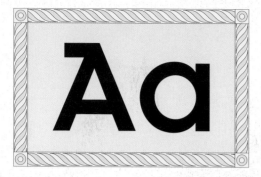

A is for alphabet.

People in Russia don't use the same letters we do to write in English. They use the Cyrillic (suh-RIH-lick) alphabet, which has 33 letters. Some Russian letters such as *H*, *K*, and *B* look like English letters, but they don't sound the same.

Fast Fact: *Two monks named Cyril and Methodius invented Russia's current alphabet in the 800s. The Cyrillic alphabet takes its name from Cyril.*

B is for ballet.

Russia is home to the two most famous ballet companies in the world, the Bolshoi Ballet and the Kirov Ballet. These two companies train children to become world-famous dancers. Hundreds of children try out for spots in these ballet schools each year, but very few are chosen.

Cc

C is for czar (ZAHR).

Russia was once ruled by czars. A czar is like a king. In the early 1900s, people were becoming unhappy with the way the czars had been ruling Russia. The czars lived with incredible riches while many others starved. Russia's last czar, Nicholas II, was forced to give up his throne in 1917.

FAST FACT: *Today, the czars' magnificent old palaces are among Russia's most famous tourist attractions.*

Czar Nicholas II

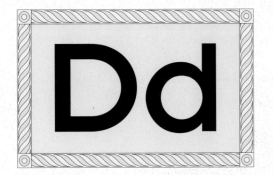

D is for doll.

Many visitors to Russia return home with beautiful hand-painted dolls. The hollow wooden dolls come stacked inside one another. As each doll is opened, a smaller one can be found inside.

These nesting dolls are called *matryoshkas* (ma-TROYSH-kahz) in Russian.

7

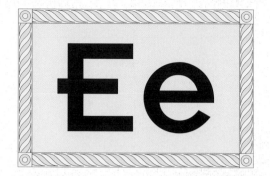

E is for Europe.

Russia's European part is much smaller than its Asian part. Yet more than three-fourths of the Russian people live in Europe. Much of Asian Russia is too cold to live in, but it is rich in natural resources, such as coal and oil.

The mountains pictured here are part of the Ural Mountain range. The Ural Mountains run north and south between European Russia and Asian Russia.

F is for flag.

The Russian flag was designed by Czar Peter the Great in 1699. It was used until 1918, after a new type of government had come to power. The new rulers, called communists, designed a different flag. When the communists left power in 1991, the country went back to this original three-striped flag.

FAST FACT: *Some people say white stands for kindness, blue for loyalty, and red for courage.*

Gg

G is for Grandfather Frost.

Grandfather Frost is a symbol of Russia's most important holiday, New Year's Day. Russian children believe Grandfather Frost brings them gifts on this day. Grandfather Frost looks a lot like Santa Claus. He drives a sleigh led by horses, and a snow maiden helps him give out gifts.

FAST FACT: *Some Russians celebrate New Year's Day twice—on January 1 and January 14. Before 1918, Russia used a different system for keeping track of months and years. According to this old system, January 14 is New Year's Day.*

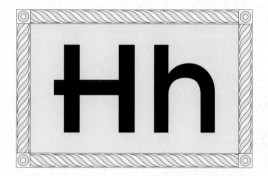

H is for hockey.

Russians love to both play and watch hockey. Many top Russian hockey players move to the United States and Canada to play for National Hockey League teams. Because Russia stays cold much of the year, Russians also enjoy sports such as ice-skating and sledding. Other popular sports are soccer, basketball, volleyball, and gymnastics.

I is for icon.

Icons are portraits of saints painted on wood panels. Members of the Russian Orthodox religion use icons to help them pray. Russia's churches are full of these colorful, detailed paintings. People also display them in their homes.

FAST FACT: *Most of the churches in Russia are Russian Orthodox, a very old form of Christianity.*

J is for jeweled egg.

Peter Carl Fabergé (1846–1920) crafted jeweled eggs for Russia's czars. He painted the eggs with real gold and decorated them with rubies, emeralds, and diamonds. Today, Fabergé's relatives still create these beautiful eggs. Wealthy Russians give them as gifts on Easter.

13

K is for Kremlin.

The Kremlin is a walled structure located in the heart of Moscow, Russia's capital city. Its name means "fortress." The Kremlin was built more than 500 years ago as a center for Russia's government. Today, the office of the Russian president is still inside the Kremlin's walls.

FAST FACT: *The Kremlin holds the world's biggest bell. Named the Czar Bell, it weighs 200 tons (181,400 kilograms).*

L is for Lake Baikal.

Lake Baikal is the deepest lake in the world. It holds more water than all of the Great Lakes of North America combined. Lake Baikal is home to 2,000 kinds of plants and animals. Of these, 1,000 are found nowhere else.

FAST FACT: *Lake Baikal is as deep as 1 mile (1½ kilometers) in some places.*

15

M is for Moscow.

Moscow is the capital and largest city of Russia. More than 8 million people live here. The city is very crowded. Most people live in tiny apartments that often have just a bathroom and one or two other rooms.

FAST FACT: *During weekends and holidays, many people from Moscow spend time at their dachas (DA-kahz), small cottages usually located outside the city.*

Nn

N is for nerpa.

Nerpas are seals that live only in Lake Baikal. They are the world's only seals that live in fresh water instead of the ocean. Nerpas can stay under water for 70 minutes. Most other seals can only be under water for 20 minutes.

O is for -ovna and -ovich.

Each Russian has three names: a first name, a middle name based on his or her father's first name, and a last name. A girl's middle name ends with "ovna" or "evna." A boy's middle name ends with "ovich" or "evich." Russians usually call one another by their first and middle names only.

Olga, daughter of Roman: Olga Romanovna

Mikhail, son of Grigory: Mikhail Grigorevich

Sergei, son of Roman: Sergei Romanovich

Anna, daughter of Grigory: Anna Grigorevna

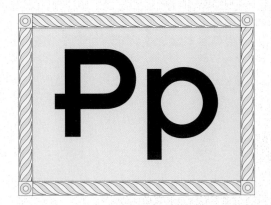

P is for piroshki.

Piroshki are small pastries stuffed with meat, vegetables, or cheese. They are often served with a beet soup called borscht. Other Russian dishes are blini (thin pancakes) and caviar (tiny fish eggs).

FAST FACT: *Most people drink tea after the main meal of the day, usually served at 1:00 in the afternoon. They sweeten their tea with jam.* **19**

Q is for queen.

In chess, each game piece has a name—and the queen is the most important piece. The Russian people, probably more than any other, love to play chess. Ordinary people play it with a passion, but Russia is also famous for producing world-class players.

FAST FACT: *The magazine* Chess Informant *asked its readers to name the top 10 chess players of the past 100 years. Four out of the 10 players named were Russian.*

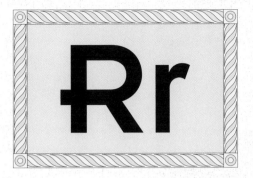

R is for ruble.

Russia's unit of money is the ruble. Rubles come in coins and bills. One ruble equals 100 kopecks. Coins range from 1 kopeck to 5 rubles. Bills go from 5 to 1,000 rubles.

Ss

S is for Saint Basil's Cathedral.

Saint Basil's Cathedral was built in the mid-1500s for Czar Ivan the Terrible. It is located near the Kremlin in Moscow. The building's colorful walls and onion-shaped domes are famous symbols of Russia.

FAST FACT: *According to legend, the cathedral's designers were blinded after the cathedral was finished. That way they could never create anything so beautiful again.*

T is for **taiga.**

A huge forested region, the taiga stretches across northern Russia. Temperatures in the taiga stay below freezing for more than six months of the year. Because of the cold weather, only a few kinds of plants can live there. But the forest is thick with dark evergreen trees, such as spruce and pine. Russians take special pride in the solemn beauty of the taiga.

FAST FACT: *Russia is home to one-fifth of the world's forests.*

U is for USSR.

From 1922 until 1991, Russia was part of an even larger country. This country was called the USSR, or the Union of Soviet Socialist Republics. The USSR was the most powerful communist country in the world. Under communist rule, everything—including land, factories, and houses—belonged to the government. When the communists lost power, the USSR broke into separate countries.

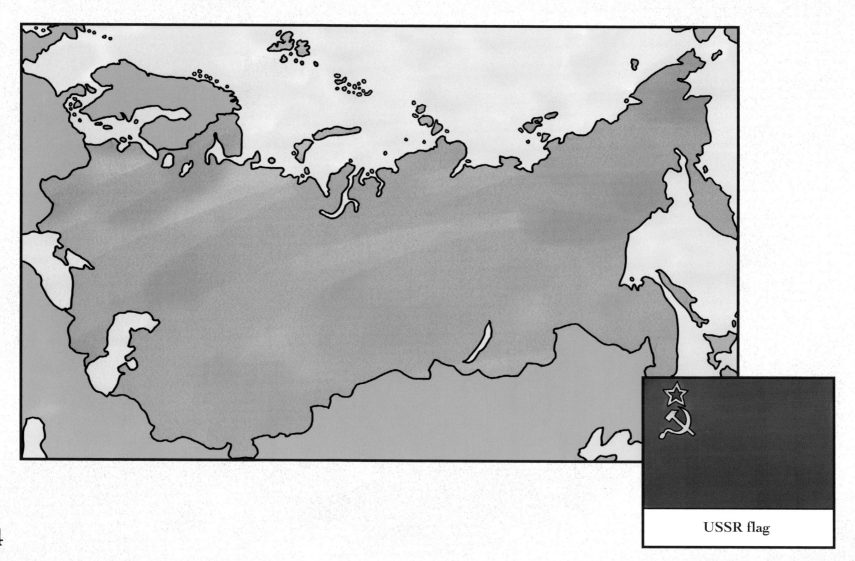

USSR flag

V is for Vladivostok.

Vv

Vladivostok is an important port city on Russia's eastern edge. It is also the last stop on the Trans-Siberian Railway. The ride across Russia from Moscow to Vladivostok takes six or seven days. But the long trip is the best way to see the country's vast and varied land.

FAST FACT: *The railroad plays an important part in Russia's economy. Instead of trucks, trains carry most of Russia's goods around the country.*

W is for White Nights.

Ww

St. Petersburg is a city in northern Russia. During the last weeks of June, the sun stays out in St. Petersburg for almost all 24 hours of the day. This special time is called White Nights. People celebrate with parties and festivals. Some people don't sleep for days at a time!

FAST FACT: On the longest day of the year, the sun doesn't set in St. Petersburg until 2:00 in the morning. It rises again just half an hour later.

X is for exports.

Russia produces large amounts of oil, natural gas, metal, and timber. The country exports these goods to other countries. Russia is the world's second largest exporter of oil.

27

Yy

Y is for Yuri Gagarin.

Yuri Gagarin, a Russian man, was the first person to go to outer space. On April 12, 1961, Gagarin orbited Earth in his spacecraft, *Vostok 1*. The whole trip took about 1 hour and 48 minutes. The first woman in space was also Russian. Valentina Tereshkova made a three-day flight in June 1963.

FAST FACT: *A Russian dog went up in space before any humans ever did! Laika orbited Earth on November 3, 1957.*

Z is for time zones.

A time zone is an area in which the same time is used. The whole earth is divided into 24 time zones. Russia is so huge it spans 11 of them. When it is noon in the westernmost part of Russia, it is 10:00 at night along the eastern edge.

FAST FACT: Russia covers about one-eighth of all the land on earth.

29

Russia in Brief

Official name: Russian Federation

Capital: Moscow (8,297,900 people)

Official language: Russian

Population: 144,526,278

People: About 83% are Russian. More than 100 ethnic minority groups make up the rest of the population.

Religion: Of those who practice a religion, 59% are Russian Orthodox, 36% are Muslim, 3% are non-Orthodox Christian, and fewer than 1% are Jewish.

Education: free for all citizens; children must attend school for at least 11 years, from ages 6 to 17

Major holidays: New Year's Day (January 1; January 14); Russian Orthodox Christmas (January 7); Soldier's Day (February 23); International Women's Day (March 8); Spring and Labor Holiday (May 1–2); Victory Day (May 9); Independence Day (June 12); Constitution Day (December 12)

Transportation: People in cities rely heavily on public transportation, including subways, buses, and trolleys. Bicycles are common in some rural areas.

Climate: varies by region; generally long, cold winters and short, mild summers

Area: 6.63 million square miles (17 million square kilometers)

Highest point: Mount Elbrus, 18,510 feet (5,642 meters) in the north Caucasus Mountains

Lowest point: coast of the Caspian Sea, 92 feet (28 meters) below sea level

Type of government: federation

Most powerful government official: president

Major industries: mining, manufacturing

Natural resources: oil, natural gas, coal, and timber

Major agricultural products: grain, sugar beets, sunflower seeds, beef, milk

Chief exports: petroleum, natural gas, wood, metals, chemicals

National symbol: double-headed eagle

Money: ruble

Say It in Russian

Russia. . . . . *roh-SEE-yah*

good-bye. . . . . *DA svee-DAH-nee-yah*

please . . . . *pah-ZAH-loo-stuh*

thank you . . . . *spa-SEE-bah*

one . . . . *ah-DIN*

two . . . . *DVAH*

three . . . . *TREE*

yes . . . . *DAH*

no . . . . *NYET*

Glossary

cathedral—a large, fancy church

caviar—tiny fish eggs often eaten on bread or crackers

chess—a board game for two players

communists—people who ruled Russia from 1918 until 1991, when it was part of the USSR

continent—one of the seven large landmasses on earth

Easter—a Christian holiday in the spring

monk—a man who lives and works in a religious community

Orthodox—belonging to a religion called Orthodoxy. Orthodoxy is a branch of Christianity.

To Learn More

At the Library

Gray, Susan H. *Russia*. Minneapolis, Minn: Compass Point Books, 2002.

Rogers, Stillman D. *Russia*. New York: Children's Press, 2002.

Thoennes, Kristin. *Russia*. Mankato, Minn.: Bridgestone Books, 2000.

On the Web

Fact Hound

Fact Hound offers a safe, fun way to find Web sites related to this book. All of the sites on Fact Hound have been researched by our staff. http://www.facthound.com

1. Visit the Fact Hound home page.
2. Enter a search word related to this book, or type in this special code: 1404802843.
3. Click on the FETCH IT button.

Your trusty Fact Hound will fetch the best sites for you!

Index